Keith Murray
DESIGNER

by
Stephen Johnson

edited by
George Perrott

A Perrot's Price Guide
GEMINI PUBLICATIONS

Published by **Gemini Publications Ltd**
30a Monmouth Street, Bath, BA1 2AN, England, UK.

Designed by Richard Gale
Jacket by Richard Gale
Illustrations by Stephen Johnson
Photography by Photoreel

ISBN 0-9530637-6-3

Printed and Bound by HSW Print.
Tel: 01443 441100.

Table *of* Contents

Acknowledgments & Credits

Andrew Casey
Andrew is an author himself on the subjects of 20th Century ceramics and kindly helped us to solve many of the problems we had compiling this book which we appreciate and thank him for.

Museums

The Wedgwood Museum
Barlaston, Stoke-on-Trent
Staffordshire, ST12 9ES, England.
Tel: +44 (0) 1782 282818
www.wedgwoodmuseum.com

Broadfield House Glass Museum
Dudley Museums Service
Compton Drive, Kingswinford,
West Midlands, DY6 9NS.
Tel: 01384 812747
Fax: 01384 812746

Royal Society of Arts
8 John Adam Street,
London, WC2N 6EZ.
Tel: 020 7451 6847

Geffrye Museum
Kingsland Road, London, E2 8EA.
Tel: 020 7739 9893

Galleries

Roland Gallery
33 Monmouth Street,
Bath, BA1 2AN.
Tel/Fax: 01225 312330
Mobile: 07889 723272
Email: therolandgallery@aol.com

FCR Gallery. 20th Century Design
58 Kensington Church Street,
London, W8 4DB.
Tel/Fax: 020 7938 5385
www.fcrgallery.com

Acknowledgments & Credits *(continued)*

Auction Houses

Potteries Specialist Auctions (PSA)
271 Waterloo Road, Cobridge,
Stoke-on-Trent, ST6 3HR.
Tel: 01782 286622
www.potteriesauctions.com

Woolley & Wallis
Salisbury Salerooms, Castle Street
Salisbury, Wiltshire, SP1 3SU.
Tel: 01772 424500, Fax: 01722 424508

Shapiro Auctioneers. Australia.
162 Queen Street,
Woollahra, NSW 2025.
Tel: 02 9326 1305, Fax: 02 9326 1305
info@shapiroauctioneers.com.au
www.shapiroauctioneers.com.au

Dealers in Art Deco wares

Odeon Art Deco
Art Deco & 20th Century Ceramics & Glass.
Email: info@odeon-artdeco.com
www.odeon-artdeco.com

Foreword

Without doubt Keith Murray was one of the most influential designers to work in the British ceramic and glass industry during the early part of the 20th century. Importantly, he looked beyond Britain to formulate his ideas on what good design should be and in particular looked to Scandinavia for inspiration.

He skilfully mixed these influences with his training as an architect to create a modern idiom for a rather conservative British market. He clearly understood that modern design had to sell in the market and knew that his work could not be too *avant garde*. This approach, coupled with the matt glazes developed by Norman Wilson at Josiah Wedgwood and Sons Ltd., proved to be an outstanding success.

His substantial achievement is all the more surprising when you consider the style of pottery and glass that was being sold at that time. The current taste is for Art Deco styled wares from the 1930s so skilfully developed by a number of manufacturers and designers such as Clarice Cliff. She successfully combined attractive patterns, often featuring stylised cottages and trees that were decorated in bold colours on geometric and angular shapes. Many of the smaller companies tried to copy the leading names and produced Art Deco styled wares that were sadly often a little too fussy and shabbily applied. In contrast, Keith Murray rejected decoration as he thought that the form should speak for itself, although he did design some stunning patterns that he felt accentuated the form such as his Cactus design for Stevens and Williams.

Keith Murray was highly regarded in the industry and soon gained an international reputation with his name soon becoming a selling point for high quality and innovative design in both glass and pottery. This much deserved status, as one of the most important designers of his day, is still as relevant today as it was back in the thirties.

Today his designs, particularly the ceramics for Wedgwood, still retain a modern look and have not dated in the slightest. His work continues to have a great appeal and in more recent years the move towards the minimalist interior has brought a renewed interest amongst design conscious people who are attracted to his simple architectural forms.

Subsequently, contemporary designers such as Nick Monro and Jasper Conran have been inspired by his great legacy to create new product lines for Wedgwood. Nick Munro used black basalt for his range of tablewares and associated items giving it a 21st century twist; whereas Jasper Conran created a stylish and simple tableware range called Casual that has proved a popular seller.

This book brings together the wide range of his work, with related information and price guide that will without doubt increase the appreciation, understanding and collectability of the pioneering designs by Keith Murray.

Andrew Casey
Specialist in decorative arts and author of
Twentieth Century Ceramic Designers in Britain.

and silver and it is in these areas that he has received recognition today.

Introduction

New Zealand born Keith Murray initially trained as an architect. During the 1930s he found it difficult to obtain work in that area and it became expedient for him to diversify his time as a designer of pottery, glass and silver and it is in these areas that he has received recognition today.

The author, Stephen Johnson, has depicted within this book the designs of Keith Murray through his work with Stevens & Williams (Glass), Josiah Wedgwood (Pottery) and Mappin & Webb (Silver Plate). Much research has gone into this book and lots of help has been kindly given in preparing the information. Establishments such as Broadfield House Glass Museum and the Wedgwood Museum have been very generous with the information they have provided, which has enabled us to display many of the shapes that Murray designed for these factories and give reference numbers to many of the important pieces that were manufactured. These reference numbers will be particularly helpful to dealers and collectors alike and it is hoped that they can be used to indicate pieces in the future.

Keith Murray was a man of his time within the British design establishment; he epitomised the Art Deco period with his simple and yet classic designs which represented modernism at its best. His ideas came from the designs of Scandinavian glass, particularly examples from Orrefors, the leading Swedish manufacturer of the time. When he visited the influential *'Exposition Internationale des Arts Décoratifs et Industriels Modernes'* in Paris in 1925, he was impressed by the complete array of modern European shapes from the Continent and felt these innovative designs should be used on British glass. It must be said that between the two Great Wars the Continentals were producing modern designs which left the British way behind in saleability; in particular the Scandanavians were producing very stylish products that Keith Murray was particularly influenced by.

Art Deco reflected both changes in the way that fashionable people lived and influences from abroad that were perceived as intriguingly exotic. The famous glass car mascots of Renê Lalique typify the styles of the day with the preoccupation for speed. The style reached its zenith at the 1925 Paris Exhibition from which the term 'Art Deco' was extracted in 1968 for an American book written by Bevis Hillier to describe the art and design movement of the era.

The most commonly collected Art Deco items in the UK are ceramic, unlike France where they favour glass such as Lalique and Gallé. The most recognisable British pottery in the Art Deco style is that of Clarice Cliff. Ceramics of this style were also made by names such as Shelley, Carlton Ware, Wade, Poole and Burleigh Ware, whereas Keith Murray is considered a designer rather than a potter. His designs at Wedgwood were another aspect of work that included architectural design. If you study the shapes of his Wedgwood pots and vases it becomes obvious that his designs are indeed of classic engineering form, which puts him in a league of his own.

This was a time in 'The Depression' when economic hardship influenced both trade and production. Traditional luxury items were unaffordable, so mass-produced replicas were made. As the 'machine aesthetic' became acceptable, more mass-produced hand finished items were made. Keith Murray recognised and accepted this but still used skilled craftspeople to finish his designs by hand.

Pieces from the 1920s were preferred to those of the 30s, and French designs were thought superior to British. However, over the past twenty or so years, ideas have levelled out and the designs of people such as Keith Murray are fetching high prices. One area that has shown increasingly more interest is glassware which has not reached its full potential yet.

The author has concentrated on the shapes and designs of Keith Murray rather than the biography of the man. He has produced a book that acquaints the reader with many of the different characteristics of Keith Murray products which will aid all those collectors and design-conscious people who are interested and deal in his wares.

George Perrott
Editor

Keith Day Pearce Murray
Biography

" I came to the conclusion that old English glass was satisfactory either when it was left plain, thereby revealing the good form of the object and the pure brilliance of the crystal, or if cut I found that I liked the well organised decoration and in particular that type of flat-cutting characteristic of Waterford which did not destroy the clarity of the glass." wrote Keith Murray in the magazine *Design for Today*.[1] In this he laid out a vision that would lead to him being recognised as one of the most important designers of his time in both glass and pottery. He worked as a freelance designer for some of the most prestigious manufacturers in their fields, Josiah Wedgwood, Stevens & Williams (which would later become Royal Brierley), and the silversmiths Mappin & Webb. Nevertheless he always considered himself an architect by vocation. It was the limited amount of work available to architects in the 1930s that led him to design the pottery, glass and silver we know him for now.

ge courtesy of Woolley & Wallis

Keith Murray was born in Auckland, New Zealand in 1892. In 1906, at the age of 14, he came to England with his parents, Charles Henry Murray, a Scot from Peterhead, and his mother, Lillian Day Murray, from Nelson, New Zealand. He was educated at Kings College, Auckland, and later at Mill Hill School, London. During the First World War he joined the Royal Flying Corps and became a pilot, to be awarded the Military Cross and the Croix de Guerre Belge. In 1921 he graduated from the London Architectural Association's School of Architecture. However, in these early days he found himself in the economic depression of the 1930s and had difficulty finding full-time work in the

[1] The article was titled "The Design of Table Glass", June 1933

architechtural field. He found some work at the architectural practice Simpson and Ayrton, with the architect Maxwell Ayrton FRIBA, and for a while taught at the Architectural Academy. He seems to have also occupied himself as a designer and illustrator, which led to an exhibition, 'Drawings of Spain', 1928, at the Lefèvre Gallery in London.[2]

Stevens & Williams

His initial inspiration for decorative art came on seeing the Swedish glass exhibited at the *Exposition des Arts Décoratifs et Industriels Modernes*, in Paris, 1925. This sought to combine the earlier Arts and Crafts Movement with industrial technology. The result was a new style of ornamentation made up of sharp, angular geometric forms and stylised natural designs. Murray found glass to be one of the most stimulating materials. He had an interest in old English glass made prior to 1850, but what he witnessed here fuelled a passion for contemporary glass work. On seeing the new forms being developed in Europe he felt that he could help to improve the quality and design of British glass.

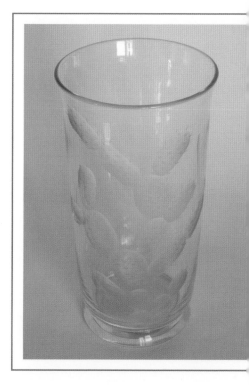

Around the time of the Swedish Industrial Art exhibition in London, 1931, Murray began to spend spare time exploring in sketchbooks the possibilities of designing glass for factory production. This eventually led to him meeting up with Marriott Powell of Whitefriars Glass Ltd to work on some experimental pieces, but little came of it and only half a dozen of Murray's designs were made. However, in 1932 he met Hubert Williams-Thomas, the Managing Director of the Stevens and Williams Glassworks, and was subsequently employed as a freelance designer for three months a year. For this he was paid about £225 plus expenses.

He learned a great deal about the techniques used in the manufacture of glassware, from the blowing of glass, to the cutting and polishing. There was

[2] A copy of the catalogue is held in the National Art Library at the Victoria and Albert Museum.

The former Royal Brierley Crystal (previously Stevens & Williams) factory at Brierley Hill, seen (in picture above) from the opposite side of the neighbouring railway track. Brierley Crystal went into receivership in 2000 which led to the manufacturing being moved to a new factory in Dudley. Parts of the old factory are in the process of demolition (as of 2004/05).

always a clear idea in his mind that the flow and form of the glass should be emphasised, and decoration only came second to this, if at all. The first examples of his new designs were displayed at the London showrooms in October 1932.

These designs were kept in a separate Description Book from the main production, intended to keep track of the new modern designs produced by the factory. The book contains around 1100 designs but it seems other designers had a few pieces included alongside. However which shapes these were was not recorded at the time.[3] There was also a number of shapes that never entered production. The exact information on which designs were actually produced, and their quantities, is not known.

[3] Reference to an unpublished interview between Roger Dodsworth and Sam Thompson, formerly of Royal Brierley, in 2001.

The range was promoted as 'Keith Murray Glass' and Reginald Williams-Thomas, the Managing Director's son, was put in charge of it. At trade fairs and for the press it was presented as a separate entity from Stevens and Williams other ranges. They were marketed primarily in London, the Home Counties, and in a few select stores elsewhere in the country, including some in Australia. Their success was judged on the prestige that resulted from their presence in exhibitions, and positive reviews in design conscious magazines like *Design for Today* and *Decorative Art, Studio Year Book.*

Many of his designs had become more decorative than the earlier sketches he produced for himself. The decorative side of the Stevens and Williams factory was thoroughly explored and utilised, experimenting with cutting, enamelling, and engraving, while still keeping it secondary to the form of the objects. He knew it

was his responsibility to produce designs that sold and made good use of the production facilities available, so he worked closely with the craftsmen as he developed them. The hand-made nature of the manufacture process was a contrast to the industrial style he often utilised.

He carried out a number of commissions in glass during this time such as the new SS Orion's glassware, and a set of glasses for the Banqueting Suite of the Royal Institute of British Architects. This collaboration between Stevens and Williams, and Murray, prospered until the outbreak of the Second World War, when he rejoined the RAF.

Mappin & Webb

With the hope of achieving a more contemporary look, the silver makers Mappin & Webb asked Murray to design some pieces for the 'British Art in Industry' Exhibition. These were only produced in small numbers and a special catalogue was produced for the show, which included cocktail sets, tea sets, and presentation cups. Unlike his pottery and glass, these did not carry either his signature or initials beside the mark. Perhaps due to the exclusivity of the medium and the traditional nature of the market, these designs were not as popular as his pottery and glass had been.

Wedgwood

In 1932, an introduction to the Manager of Josiah Wedgwood & Sons Ltd's London showroom, Felton Wreford, resulted in an invitation to the Etruria factory. After discussions with Josiah Wedgwood, Murray was invited to work for the company on a freelance basis, which he accepted. In an effort to improve their economic and artistic position following the depression, Wedgwood were commissioning a new group of artists to design for them. While the majority of these new artists designed patterns, Murray concentrated on the shape and form just as he did with glass. In this he was helped by Tom Wedgwood the cousin of Josiah, Norman Wilson the Production Manager, and Victor Skellern who in 1934 was promoted to Art Director. Keith Murray's designs were for simple tableware and decorative ware items, which included bowls, vases, cups and saucers, plates, ashtrays, cigarette boxes, and inkwells.

Upon joining Wedgwood he was asked to assist with the design of a dinner service for Rouard of Paris, which Tom Wedgwood and John Goodwin had already begun. Specifically, he was to help with the design of the vegetable tureens. This dinner service was named 'Annular'. Today some people make the mistake of assuming that Murray designed all the Annular ware. The tureens which Murray designed for the set were modelled and put into production later in 1932.

Murray was now working for Wedgwood for forty eight working days per year, for the sum of £125, along with retainer and royalties. He was fortunate that the then Works Manager, Norman Wilson, had been since 1927 developing many new glazes, which Murray used on his designs. These included the moonstone,

Image courtesy of Woolley & Wallis

matt green, straw, duck egg blue, champagne, and copper basalt. However a number of wares with the matt champagne glaze were withdrawn as they were unfortunately prone to scratch too easily on contact with silver tableware.

Keith Murray's wares were first shown at the British Art in Relation to the Home Exhibition in London, 1933. Then soon after, at the Exhibition of New Wedgwood Shapes held at John Lewis's in Oxford Street, London. 124 new Murray designs were on show, including a number of unique wares. The combination of these ceramics and the glassware that he was designing for the Stevens & Williams company, soon led to Murray becoming one of Europe's pioneering designers. He won a gold medal at the fifth Milan Triennale, in 1933. Major exhibitions were now showing examples of his work, including the Royal Academy's exhibition, 'British Art in Industry' in 1935, 'Britain Can Make It' at the V&A in 1946, and Royal Designers for Industry's exhibition 'Design at Work' in 1948.

Images courtesy of Odeon Art Deco

In 1935 there was also a one-man show of his designs at The Medici Galleries in London which covered his pottery, glass and silver designs.

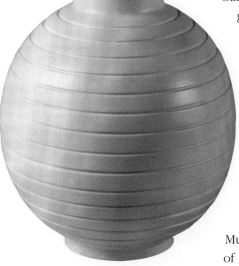

Keith Murray had a modernist belief in simplified, and yet classical, hand-worked forms, emphasizing the inherent beauty. His designs were a compromise between mass-production and the skill involved in their manufacture. Often they sold well and so were produced in fairly large quantities. Interestingly many of these designs were not initially big sellers. The trade press began to praise Keith Murray highly and before long he become one of Wedgwood's most popular designers.

Image courtesy of J. Wedgwood & Sons Ltd

A number of hand painted patterns were designed by Murray from 1934 that could be cheaply produced upon Wedgwood's dinner and tea sets. These patterns included Lotus, Weeping Willow (also called Green Tree), Iris, Radio, Tulip, Wheat Border, Pink Flower and Pink & Red Pimpernel. From 1936, a range of cheaper slip cast wares were also introduced which allowed a quicker production time.

Image courtesy of J. Wedgwood & Sons Ltd

Other artists at Wedgwood used some of Murray's shapes in designing their own patterns, in particular Millicent Taplin's silver lustre designs. Later, otherwise plain mugs would be produced with transfers of company logos or university crests.

Perhaps Murray's biggest job for Wedgwood was the design of the new factory at Barlaston. He had resumed his architectural practice in 1936, forming his own firm, Ramsey, Murray and White. With his partner, Charles White, they designed the factory and production workshops, while an independent architect, Louis de Soissons, designed a model village and the general layout of the estate.

Work began on the new building in 1939 with the first section being completed in 1940, one year into the Second World War. Sadly, due to the restrictions imposed during the War, important changes had to be made which would alter the look of Wedgwood's new building. Murray's original plans were for a modernist white facade. This had to be replaced with ordinary red brick.

For his last big ceramic commission at Wedgwood, Murray was asked in 1946 to produce a brand new table service to be named the Commonwealth Service. It was a basic body shape that could either carry a variety of Wedgwood patterns, or remain attractive as undecorated utility ware.

Image courtesy of Woolley & Wallis

Image courtesy of Odeon Art Deco

Weeping Willow, aka Green Tree
AL 9679

Iris
AMH 9613

Lotus
(russet red and bronze) - **S. 70**
(green and silver) - **S203**

The Commonwealth Service in an achive photograph from J. Wedgwood and Sons Ltd, 1947-8

Royal Designer for Industry

In 1936, Murray was awarded the distinction of Royal Designer for Industry by The Royal Society for the encouragement of Arts, Manufacturers & Commerce, and was on the list of the first twelve recipients. He became Master of the RDI Faculty between 1945-47. During his time with the RDI, he would have helped with the selection of members, been involved in debates about by-laws, and there is a record of him as member of the assessors on a design competition for a drinking fountain.[4]

Murray left Wedgwood in 1948, although his designs were still in production during the 1950s. He could now concentrate on working as an architect. In 1939 he was elected a fellow of the Royal Institute of British Architects, and with the war now over architects were in demand. Murray's business was becoming increasingly busy. The practice changed its name to Ramsey, Murray, White and Ward, on the joining of Basil Ward. Their offices were based above the Wedgwood showrooms on Wigmore Street, London, accumulating over 30 employees. They specialised in commercial and industrial buildings, as well as airports, notable

Image courtesy of J. Wedgwood & Sons Ltd

---

[4] The archives of the the RSA holds a number of documents and correspondence relating to Keith Murray's involvement with them.

examples being concrete hangers at London Airport and the Hong Kong airport built in the 1950s.

He retired from the practice in 1967, and briefly returned to the Wedgwood factory to be presented with a large black basalt bowl decorated in gold lettering.[5] He died in May 1981, aged 89.

The Victoria and Albert Museum in London organised a touring exhibition on Keith Murray in 1976, which after a period of neglect, brought him back into the public eye. This was followed by inclusion in the 'British Glass Between the Wars' exhibition at Broadfield House Glass Museum, 1987, and a retrospective exhibition in 2001. There was also an exhibition in 1996 in his native New Zealand which has in recent times reclaimed him as their own. All of this has helped bring back his popularity, and led to the rapid increase in the auction prices of his designs.

Keith Murray was a true modernist; his work was pure in its simplicity, and did not suffer the gaudiness that other ceramic designers followed in order to be different. His work is represented in major museums in the UK and around the world, including the Victoria and Albert in London, Broadfield House Glass Museum in the West Midlands, the Museum of London, the Brighton Museum, the Walker in Liverpool, and the National Gallery of Victoria in Australia. This alone shows his reputation as a designer. As one of the mid-twentieth century's leading art critics, Herbert Read (also champion of another great modernist, Henry Moore), said "The Beer Mugs designed by Keith Murray are better than anything else in modern English ceramics."

Image courtesy of Odeon Art Deco

[5] Courtesy of Andrew Casey in his book 20th Century Ceramic Designers in Britain

Image courtesy of Odeon Art Deco

Pottery Bodies & Glazes

Queensware was a fine cream-white earthenware developed by Josiah Wedgwood, which was less expensive than the porcelain being produced at the time. In 1765 he was commissioned to produce a tea service for Queen Charlotte, who was so pleased with the result she gave him permission to rename the cream earthenware Queensware after herself.

When Norman Wilson became Works Manager of the Etruria factory in 1927, he headed a team dedicated to modernisation and expansion. An imaginative experimenter, sound technician, and with a strong grasp of good business practice, he pioneered many new bodies and glazes. The majority of Keith Murray's ceramic designs made use of Queensware in these newly developed glazes.

The moonstone, matt green, matt straw, duck-egg blue and champagne clear glaze were the most used with Keith Murray's designs, although after 1940 only moonstone, matt green, and matt straw remained in use.

Image courtesy of Odeon Art Deco

Basalt

Basalt was a stoneware body developed by Josiah Wedgwood in 1767. He created the formula to resemble an igneous rock used in Egyptian art called Basaltes. This succeeded to such a degree that he described it as "a fine porcelain bisque, of nearly the same properties as the natural stone, it receives a high polish, serves as a touchstone for metals, strikes fire with steel, resists all the acids, and bears without injury, a stronger fire than basalts itself." The cut is noticeably sharper and cleaner than with Queensware.

Norman Wilson and his team added their own variation to this basalt, including a dry red body known as Copper or Bronze Basalt. Both Black Basalt and the Copper Basalt were in use until 1940. After this point it seems that mainly Black Basalt was used. These Basalt wares were more expensive to produce, so retailed at a higher price than the Queensware.

Image courtesy of Bridgman Art Library

Slipware

Slipware is a pottery on which a thin layer of slip clay has been applied onto the surface of an earthenware pot. The slip is a clay that has been mixed with water until it is about the thickness of cream. This method of decoration goes as far back as Roman and Mediaeval times, though only became fully exploited in the 17th century.

Keith Murray designed his slipware pieces around 1936 in a distinctive two-colour effect. These use a cream earthenware body that has been hand thrown on a wheel, then dipped in a slip clay that gives it a layer of contrasting colour. Finally it is dried before cutting on the lathe, where the colour of the lower layer is revealed.

Pottery Marks

Keith Murray
WEDGWOOD
MADE IN ENGLAND
MATT GREEN

By 1932 Keith Murray was given the rare honour of a stamp with his signature alongside the usual Wedgwood name.

Sometimes the words MOONSTONE, MATT GREEN, or MATT STRAW can also be seen.

For the Basalt, where a black stamp would be lost, a red version was used. A smaller stamp with only the initials KM was also produced in 1934.

KM
WEDGWOOD
MADE IN ENGLAND

Wedgwood impressed letters and numbers refer to the potter and date of manufacture, usually in the format of month, potter, year. Wedgwood had from 1860 to 1929 used code letters for all three. From 1930 the actual date was applied on the wares, first as the month, then a letter to represent the potter, and finally the last two figures of the year, i.e. 3B35 = March 1935 and later simply as two figures i.e. 57 = 1957. Sometimes workman's errors occur, and also the letters are not always legible. Handpainted pieces also carry a painted pattern number.

OF ETRURIA
KM
WEDGWOOD
MADE IN ENGLAND
BARLASTON

As earthenware production transferred to Barlaston in 1940 the circle stamp came into use. This has often been used as a method of dating pieces, although cannot be one hundred percent relied on. Although the circular stamp only came after 1940, sometimes later pieces have been found with the an earlier stamp.

It is not unusual to discover wares by Keith Murray without marks, so familiarity with the shapes are as important when buying.

Murray designed a number of commemorative pieces and his mark was adapted for these pieces. The example illustrated was used on the mug shape 3810.

By Courtesy of the Trustees of the Wedgwood Museum, Barleston, Stoke-on-Trent, Staffordshire, England.

Glass Marks

For Stevens & Williams, Murray's mark again was his signature, acid etched above the Stevens & Williams mark.

It was common for the glass signature to be missing. While it might have been forgotten during production, is also likely that certain sellers requested unmarked pieces. Sometimes it was etched too faintly and the mark became obscured through wear and tear.

Wedgwood Shapes

From the time he started working with Wedgwood until at least the late 1950s Keith Murray's designs were produced in a variety of bodies, glazes and sizes. Many were made in large quantities, but others only in small numbers. There was also the occasional experimental shape or glaze that did not make it into full production.

Here we endeavour to give an overview of the shapes he designed. This is not an authorative list of all his designs. Many of these designs were listed in the Wedgwood catalogue *Bodies, Glazes and Shapes Current for 1940-1950*. The Annular ware has not been included.

Please note that the colours used in these illustrations are only an example and may not have been used on all shapes. This list should be used as a guide only.

Wedgwood Shapes

Ashtray
3881

Matt Glazes

Ashtray
4107

Matt Glazes

Ashtray
4117

Matt Glazes

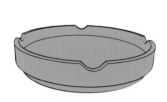

Ashtray
4253

Slipware

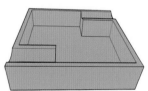

Ashtray
4329

Matt Glazes

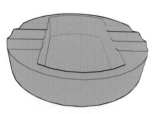

Ashtray
4330

Matt Glazes

Bath Salts Jar
4125

Matt Glazes

Beaker
3884

Basalt

Beaker
3885

Basalt

Wedgwood Shapes

Beaker	Bookends	Bowl
3888	**Number not known**	**3753**
Basalt	Matt Glazes	Matt Glazes

Bowl	Bowl	Bowl
3806	**3807**	**3813**
Matt Glazes	Matt Glazes	Matt Glazes + Basalt

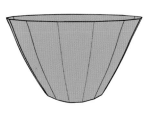

Bowl	Bowl	Bowl
3815	**3819**	**3993**
Matt Glazes + Basalt	Matt Glazes	Matt Glazes

Wedgwood Shapes

Bowl	Bowl	Bowl
3994	**3995**	**4020**
Matt Glazes	Matt Glazes	Matt Glazes

Bowl	Bowl	Bowl
4116	**4118**	**4119**
Matt Glazes	Matt Glazes	Matt Glazes

Bowl	Bowl	Bowl
4126	**4129**	**4194**
Matt Glazes	Matt Glazes	Slipware

Wedgwood Shapes

Bowl
4199
Slipware

Bowl
4200
Slipware

Bowl
4218
Slipware

Bowl
4222
Slipware

Bowl
4223
Slipware

Bowl
4226
Slipware

Bowl
4227
Slipware

Bowl
4245
Slipware

Bowl
4251
Slipware

Wedgwood Shapes

Bowl	Bowl	Bowl
4254	**4319**	**4322**
Slipware	Matt Glazes	Matt Glazes

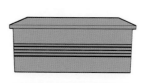

Box, Cigarette	Box, Cigarette	Box, Cigarette
3871	**3872**	**4112**
Matt Glazes	Matt Glazes	Matt Glazes

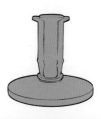

Box, Denture	Box, Sugar	Candlestick
4114	**3901**	**4108**
Matt Glazes	Matt Glazes + Basalt	Matt Glazes

Wedgwood Shapes

Cocktail Cups	Coffee Pot	Comport
3999	**3901**	**4120**
Matt Glazes	Matt Glazes + Basalt	Matt Glazes

Compotier	Cream	Cup and Saucer
4121	**3901**	**3901**
Matt Glazes	Matt Glazes + Basalt	Matt Glazes

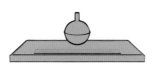

Honey, Notched	Inkstand	Inkstand
4382	**Number not known**	**3873**
Matt Glazes	Matt Glazes	Matt Glazes

Wedgwood Shapes

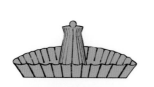 

Inkstand	Inkstand	Jar, Cigarette
4110	**4131**	**4252**
Matt Glazes	Matt Glazes	Slipware

Jar, Tobacco	Jar, Tobacco	Jar, Tobacco
3862	**3865**	**4111**
Basalt	Basalt	Matt Glazes

Jug	Jug	Jug
3822	**3844**	**3845**
Matt Glazes	Matt Glazes	Matt Glazes

Wedgwood Shapes

Jug
3974

Matt Glazes

Jug
4193

Slipware

Lamp Vase
3955

Matt Glazes

Lamp Vase
3956

Matt Glazes

Mug
Number not known

Matt Glazes

Mug
3810

Matt Glazes

Mug
3970

Matt Glazes

Mug
3971

Matt Glazes

Mug
3974

Matt Glazes

Wedgwood Shapes

Mug	Plate, Dessert	Powder Bowl
4192	**4122**	**4113**
Slipware	Matt Glazes	Matt Glazes

Tray	Tumbler	Vase
3812	**4115**	**3765**
Matt Glazes	Matt Glazes	Matt Glazes

Vase	Vase	Vase
3801	**3802**	**3805**
Matt Glazes	Matt Glazes	Matt Glazes

Wedgwood Shapes

Vase
3808
Matt Glazes

Vase
3816
Basalt

Vase
3818
Basalt

Vase
3820
Matt Glazes

Vase
3842
Matt Glazes

Vase
3868
Matt Glazes + Basalt

Vase
3869
Basalt

Vase
3870
Matt Glazes + Basalt

Vase
3877
Basalt

Wedgwood Shapes

Vase
3882
Basalt

Vase
3890
Basalt

Vase
3891
Basalt

Vase
3985
Matt Glazes

Vase
3986
Matt Glazes

Vase
3987
Matt Glazes

Vase
3988
Matt Glazes

Vase
3990
Matt Glazes

Vase
3991
Matt Glazes + Basalt

Wedgwood Shapes

Vase

3992

Matt Glazes

Vase

4014

Matt Glazes

Vase

4061

Matt Glazes + Basalt

Vase

4062

Matt Glazes + Basalt

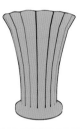

Vase

4124

Matt Glazes

Vase

4128

Matt Glazes

Vase

4130

Matt Glazes

Vase

4195

Slipware

Vase

4196

Slipware

Wedgwood Shapes

Vase
4197
Slipware

Vase
4198
Slipware

Vase
4215
Slipware

Vase
4216
Slipware

Vase
4217
Slipware

Vase
4219
Slipware

Vase
4220
Slipware

Vase
4225
Slipware

Vase
4244
Slipware

Wedgwood Shapes

Vase

4248

Slipware

Vase

4249

Slipware

Vase

4314

Matt Glazes

Vase

4315

Matt Glazes

Vase

4316

Matt Glazes

Vase

4317

Matt Glazes

Vase

4318

Matt Glazes

Vase

4320

Matt Glazes

Vase

4321

Matt Glazes

Wedgwood Shapes

Vase

4323

Matt Glazes

Vase

4324

Matt Glazes

Vase

4325

Matt Glazes

Vase

4326

Matt Glazes

Wall Vase

4141

Matt Glazes

Keith Murray Description Book

The only record of the variety of glass that Keith Murray designed is in KM Description Book currently looked after by the Broadfield House Glass Museum. Stevens & Williams kept the Keith Murray Description Book as a record of their new modern designs. It is believed that because it was intended to record modern designs, a few by other designers were included, however it is difficult now to know which pieces these are.

The book is a folder of loose leaf pages with drawings of the designs with numbers at the side of the page. As the pieces were designed, they would be drawn for the book and calculations made for costing. It was necessary to work out the number that could be made in six hours, their weight, and how long the decoration would take. This would often be written at the side. All patterns were then given a number ending with an A, and running from 100 to 1198.

Keith Murray made full use of the many techniques available at Stevens & Williams. This resulted in a huge variety of designs.

Description Book

Keith Murray Description Book

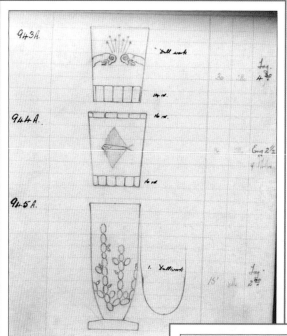

Sample pages from the Keith Murray Description Book which records the designs produced by Keith Murray for Stevens & Williams between 1932 and 1939.

The book comes in a loose-leaf format so that extra pages could be added as new designs were created. Pattern numbers begin at 100 and go up to 1198, indicating that in his seven years at Stevens & Williams Murray produced over 1000 designs.

(Reproduced by courtesey of Broadfield House Glass Museum, Kingswinford)

Situated in the historic Stourbridge glassmaking district, Broadfield House Glass Museum contains an unrivalled collection of 19th and 20th century Stourbridge glass, including a number of pieces by Keith Murray. Researchers and serious collectors of Keith Murray glass are advised to make an appointment as not all the collection is on permanent display.

For further information telephone 01384 812745 or visit www.glassmuseum.org.uk

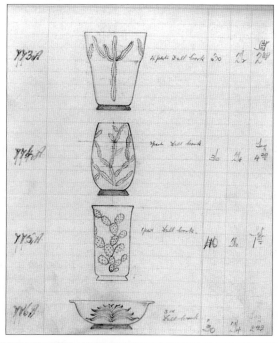

Keith Murray Description Book

The following extracts are taken from conversations with Sam Thompson, who worked in the Drawing Office at Stevens & Williams. Thompson was aged 91 at the time of these conversations and his recollections may not be entirely accurate. However in the absence of other first-hand information about the book, his comments are worth publishing.

The Keith Murray book was known as the Keith Murray Description Book. It was drawn up to provide a handy record of all the Keith Murray designs that were put into production during his time at Stevens & Williams (1932-1939) and to record information that would enable those designs to be costed.

The book was compiled over the period of time that Murray was with Stevens & Williams, hence the loose-leaf format. As each design was finalised and accepted, it was given a pattern number, drawn into the book and its production details recorded in columns to the right of the drawing. All the pieces in the book were put into production in one form or other, otherwise they wouldn't have been entered in the book.

The production details that were critical for costing and which were recorded in the book were:

1. Number of pieces that could be made in six hours;
2. Weight of article before decoration;
3. Length of time it took for decoration to be carried out.

By recording these details the factory had accurate information on which to base its initial costing and any subsequent revision to price.

The designs were drawn into the book by Sam Thompson and Tom Jones who worked in the drawing office at Stevens & Williams. They are not Murray's drawings.

Not all the designs in the book are by Keith Murray. The book was used to record modern-style designs by other members of the Stevens & Williams staff such as Hubert and Reginald Silvers Williams-Thomas. The designs which Sam Thompson knows are not Murray have been annotated by him in biro "Not K.M." If the

Description Book

company had known how significant Murray was to become, they would not have included non-Murray designs in the book.

Not all the shapes are by Murray. He made use of some existing Stevens & Williams shapes.

Patterns numbers were given the suffix 'A' in order to distinguish them from any existing Stevens & Williams numbers. The numbers were started at 100 to make it look as though the Keith Murray range was already well established. There were never any numbers before 100. There was only one Keith Murray Description Book. There was never a book B.

Any additional numbers in the book may have been estimate numbers. These were like temporary numbers that design was given while it was being trialed, costed and considered for production.

Some customers, eg China Craft, did not want the Keith Murray/S&W mark on the glass, which explains why some KM glass is not marked.

Book was kept in the Drawing Office and was not used by the glassmakers or decorators. They would work from full-scale drawings.

Roger Dodsworth
Broadfield House Glass Museum
July/August 2001

Affordable Coloured Glass

Clear glass was used and also a variety of other colours including bottle green, amber, pale blue, and smokey black. Murray's architectural training led him to think about the way a design could be used as much as its appearance. He had also seen how mass production could enable more copies to be produced at less cost. These influences combined when he saw the contemporary Swedish glass. They were producing beautiful and elegant glassware at prices which an average person could afford. Stevens & Williams on the other hand were dedicated to their skilled hand craftsmen, so were resistant to modernisation which might put production and jobs at risk, and never produced at a price to rival the Swedish output. However, Murray still preferred designs of undecorated and well formed glass. These would often be blown using a mould, and so be made at the lowest price possible.

303A   Number not known   Number not known

Designs

Designs ranged from simple elegant table services and sherry sets often in colourless crystal to drinking sets in coloured glass, and ornamental glass in crystal, coloured or two-coloured glass.

Clear glass with a black foot and stopper was common to Art Deco glassware, especially Swedish glassware, and Keith Murray worked on a number of similar pieces, including one set with a black spiral threaded around the body.

422A   425A   457A

Blown Glass

Blown glass is one of the oldest of all glass making techniques, the simplicity of it was well suited to Keith Murray. His clear sense of form was brought out with elegance, achieving symmetry and smoothness.

The basic free-blowing process begins with a gather of molten glass attached to the blowing iron and blown into. This might then be spun until an even surface is formed, when it is transferred to a pontil iron to be shaped. The glass now with it's final shape and size, is removed from the rod and left to slowly cool down.

Many designs would also need to be dipped into a mould. These would allow optic effects such a rippling or bubble patterns to be formed.

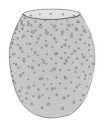

| 860A | 1147A | 1060A Green |

Cut Glass

A number of architectural cut glass pieces were designed early on by Murray. These had a mechanistic feel to them and would have taken a long time to cut, thus making them very expensive.

Besides these, Murray also tried to update the conservative nature of Stevens & Williams' earlier cut glass, whilst making use of traditional patterns such as reverse diamonds and broad flutes. For these he would use simple and elegant shapes with just enough being cut to complement the form.

| 521A | 683A | 437A |

Engraved Glass

The engraved cactus glass is Keith Murray's most famous and recognisable design in glass and was adapted in a number of variations. The naturalistic plant motif was usually central to the shape and required a great deal of skill from the engraver. Stevens and Williams were keen for Murray to develop decorative pieces like this for their craftsmen. Besides the cacti he also designed engraved motifs of other fauna, fish amongst bubbles and weeds, and a complex airport design. These detailed engravings are recorded in the design book alongside simpler patterns that repeat either all-over or around borders. These made use of stars, flowers, or geometric motifs.

Examples from
Mappin *&* **Webb**

The silversmiths Mappin & Webb produced a small number of designs by Keith Murray especially for the 'British Art in Industry' exhibition in 1935. As they were not known for modern design, this was calculated to guarantee their place in the exhibition and to gain an edge over their rivals. The designs include presentation cups, cocktail sets, bowls, tea service, tankard, and an electroplate casserole dish. Mappin & Webb also produced an illustrated catalogue for the exhibition.

Examples of these designs were also displayed at the 'Glass, Pottery and Silver designed by Keith Murray' show at the Medici Galleries. Although these pieces continued to be sold after the show, they were not produced in large numbers as the silver market remained relatively traditional, as well as expensive, so they are rare today.

Examples from Mappin & Webb

Ceramics

PRICE GUIDE

Our **Valuation** *Policy*

This is a new publication and we have priced the individual pieces from recent sales at either English auction houses or from the internet. This information is shown on the individual items within the book which helps the collector to see what prices have been made during the past year.

Generally you cannot take an individual sale at auction or on the internet and expect that price to be the valuation of that particular piece; prices can be high or low according to the condition of the piece and the amount of bidders that want that particular item, so with that in mind we have decided to show an estimated spread valuation. i.e. £100-150. being an average price of the lower and higher end of the market. Obviously, these are estimated prices and individual buyers and sellers will use their own discretion.

Most auction houses add 'buyers commission' which is added to the sale price; it can differ from 10 to 19.5 percent plus VAT at any particular auction. In consideration of this, we have averaged a 20 per cent increase in this price guide on all auction prices where we believe this has taken place.

Ground colours of the Wedgwood wares can make a difference in the value of a piece. Generally, Moonstone, Matt Green and Matt Straw are around the same price to collectors; the colour Blue is a little more collectable whereas Grey, which was produced in smaller numbers can be more desirable and fetch higher prices. Black Basalt is a more expensive colour and usually fetches more than double the other colours, but the most valuable and collectable of them all is Bronze Basalt.

We were not able to match photographs with every sale and valuation we list here, so where this has been a problem we tried to include a photograph of the same design in a different colour.

Vases

Price Guide

Vase 3765

Moonstone, 18.5cm (7.5") high.
Woolley & Wallis Sept 2003
sold £300
Ebay Dec 2004 sold £361
Est. £450-600

Moonstone, 24cm (9.5") high.
Diamond Mills & Co. Jun 2004
sold £420
Ebay Mar 2005 sold £470
Est. £600-750

Matt Green, 18.5cm (7.5") high.
Sworders Dec 2003 sold £210
Est. £450-600

Matt Green, 24cm (9.5") high.
PSA Sept. 2004 sold £290
Ebay Mar 2005 sold £360
Est. £600-750

BOMB VASES

This design was made in four sizes and in various colours: straw, white, moonstone, and green. Blue and grey are rarer and more collectable.

Vase 3765

Matt Straw, 18.5 cm (7.5") high.
Woolley & Wallis Apr 2004
sold £220
Ebay Oct 2004 sold £226
Est. £450-600

Matt Straw, 24 cm (9.5") high.
Sotheby's Jun 1999 sold £340
Est. £600-750

Blue, 15.75 cm (6") high.
Dreweatt Neate Donnington Jun 2003
sold £380
Christies Feb. 2004 sold £360
Est. £550-750

Blue, 19 cm (7.5") high.
Woolley & Wallis Nov 2003
sold £360
Ebay Oct 2004 sold £550
Est. £650-850

Blue, 23.5 cm (9.5") high.
Louis Taylor Fine Art Jun 2002
sold £540
Law Fine Art Feb 2004 sold £450
Est. £750-900

This grey glaze is relatively rare in the Keith Murray range. Apparently the colour had a limited use and was withdrawn in c.1940.

Vase 3801

Matt Straw, 16cm (6.5") high.
Woolley & Wallis Apr 2004 sold £190
Ebay Mar 2005 sold £245
Est. £300-400

Moonstone (not pictured), 16cm (6.5") high.
Sworders Jun 2003 sold £180
Ebay Feb 2005 sold £181
Est. £300-400

Matt Green, 16cm (6.5") high.
Fellows & Sons Oct 2003 sold £190
Ebay Dec 2004 sold £180
Est. £300-400

Blue, (not pictured), 15cm (6") high.
Ebay May 2005 sold £463
Est. £650-800

Grey, 14.5cm (5.5").
Sworders Apr 2003 sold £400
Est. £650-800

Vase 3802

Straw, 22 cm (8.5") high.
Est. £1000-1500

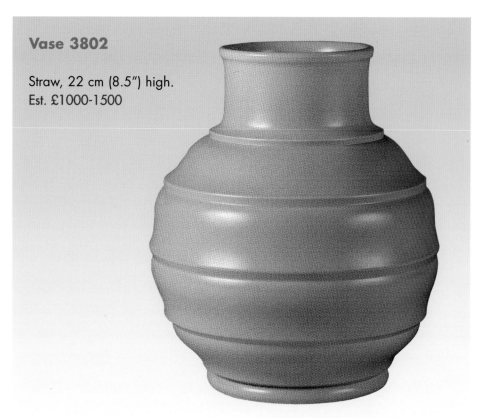

This particular vase has an unusual shape that is similar to the vase numbered 3765. While the earlier vase is quite common this shape has become much rarer. Without placing these shapes side by side it would be possible to mistake one for the other. These spherical shapes are often described as being bomb vases or football vases.

Condition

- The condition of a piece is the most important thing to look at before you purchase.
- Good condition is essential, especially with monochrome glazes.
- Slight damage underneath the base is acceptable, as are slight kiln digs.
- Restoration should not be acceptable, even good restoration. The only time when it is acceptable is when a piece is very, very, rare.
- Sometimes the interiors of bowls and vases have discolouration or fading where water was used in them.
- All faults and blemishes should always be reflected in the price, whether the piece is common or rare.

Vase 3805

Matt Green,
29cm (11.5") high.
*Sotheby's Nov 2001
sold £470
Ebay Nov 2004 sold £565*
Est. £750-950

Blue, 29 cm (11.5") high.
*Woolley & Wallis Apr 2004 sold £360
Christies Feb 2005 sold £360*
Est. £750-950

Matt Straw, 28.5 cm (11") high.
PSA Sept 2004 sold £400
Est. £750-950

Moonstone,
28.5 cm (11") high.
*Bonhams Feb 2004
sold £478
Ebay Mar 2005 sold £970*
Est. £750-950

Image provided courtesy of Shapiro Auctioneers.
From Left 3818, 3813, 3816.

Vase 3816

Black Basalt, 20.5 cm (8") high.
Shapiro Sept 2004 sold AU$2640/£1073
Ebay Mar 2005 sold £1298
Est. £1500-2000

Vase 3818

Black Basalt, 20.5 cm (8") high.
Shapiro Sept 2004
sold AU$2640/£1070
Ebay Feb 2005 sold £1915
Est. £1700-2200

Vase 3820

Matt Green, 17 cm (6.5") high.
Shapiro Sept 2004
sold AU$3840/£1561
Est. £1000-1400

Blue, 17 cm (6.5") high.
Christies Feb 2005 sold £600
Ebay Mar 2005 sold £839
Woolley & Wallace May 2005
sold £750
Est. £1200-1600

Vase 3808

Moonstone, 19 cm (7.5") high.
Woolley & Wallis May 2005
sold £170
Est. £300-400

Engine-turned Vases

Few of Murray's vases were suitable for mass-production. Many pieces were hand-thrown and then finished on an engine-turned lathe to give the characteristic ridges which are typical on the designs of 'bomb' vases.

Vase 3842

Moonstone, 24 cm (9.5") high.
Shapiro Sept 2004 sold AU$1200/£489
Ebay May 2005 sold £365
Est. £600-850

Vase 3868

Moonstone,
12 cm (4.75") high.
Ebay Apr 2005 sold £242
Est. £450-650

Image provided courtesy of Shapiro Auctioneers.

Back Row from Left 3842, 3805, 3842.
Front Row from Left 3801, 3808, 3872, 3765, 4318.

Vase 3870

Matt Green (not pictured), 15 cm (5.75") high.
PSA Sept. 2004 sold £230
Ebay Jan 2005 sold £280
Est. £350-550

Blue (not pictured), 15 cm (5.75") high.
Cheffins Apr 2005 sold £200
Est. £350-550

Black Basalt, 14 cm (5.5") high.
Bonhams Feb 2004 sold £896
Christies Feb 2005 sold £720
Est. £1200-1500

Vase 3988

Moonstone, 15.5 cm (6") high.
Ebay Mar 2005 sold £770
Est. £1000-1300

Colours included matt green, moonstone, matt straw.
Blue, grey and champagne were used up to c.1940.

Vase 3891

Black Basalt, 22 cm (8.75") high.
McTear's Apr 2004 sold £1350
Est. £1700-2200

Vase 3869

Est. £1200-1500

Basalt Vase. Many Murray shapes were made in black basalt by Wedgwood in traditional materials but a new copper-coloured basalt was introduced in 1933.

Basalt

Basalt wares have been produced by Wedgwood since the 19th century but it was in the 1930s that it was first used for Keith Murray shapes. Many wares were made by using the traditional techniques of being thrown and then finished off by turning and cutting on a lathe. Black and bronze basalt vases are considered the most collectable pieces from the Keith Murray range, with bronze being the rarer.

Vase 3882

Black Basalt, 20.5 cm (8") high.
Est. £1700-2200

Vase 3991

Bronze Basalt, 22 cm (8.75") high.
Christies Feb 2005
sold £1200 top rim restored
Est. £2000-3000

Vase 3991

Moonstone, 23 cm (9") high.
Ebay Mar 2005 sold £155
Woolley & Wallis May 2005 sold £150
Est. £300-400

Matt Green, 15.5 cm (6") high.
Est. £300-400

Vase 4124

Blue, 21 cm (8.5") high.
Ebay Apr 2005 sold £282
Est. £350-500

Vase 4124
Matt green
Est. £350-500

Vase 4128

Moonstone, 19 cm
(7.5") high.
Est. £450-650

Vase 4130

Matt Green.
Est. £350-500

Price Guide

Vase 4197

Celadon Slipware.
Ebay Nov 2004 sold £272
Ebay Dec 2004 sold $433/£231
Est. £400-500

Vase 4198

Celadon Slipware,
21.5 cm (8.5") high.
Est. £250-400

Vase 4225

Celadon Slipware
Ebay Nov 2004 sold £77
Est. £150-200

Vase 4215

Celedon Slipware, 18.5 cm (7.25") high.
Woolley & Wallis Feb 2004 sold £220
Ebay Feb 2005 sold £224
Est. £300-450

Champagne Slipware
(not pictured),
18.5 cm (7.25") high.
Law Fine Art Jan 2003 sold £160
Est. £300-450

Vase 4217

Celadon Slipware, 20 cm (8") high.
Cheffins Apr 2004 sold £130
Woolley & Wallis May 2005
sold £220
Est. £300-450

Vase 4248

Celadon Slipware, 21cm (8.25") high.
Ebay Apr 2005 sold £45
Ebay Apr 2005 sold £72
Est. £150-200

Celadon Slipware, 25cm (10") high.
PSA Sept. 2004 sold £75
Ebay Dec 2004 sold £100
Est. £150-200

These urns and similar pieces of the slipware range were made by traditional methods using different-colour clays. Usually celadon green with cream or champagne with ivory.

Vase 4314

Moonstone, 19 cm (7.5") high.
Ebay May 2005 sold £190
Est. £350-450

Vase 4315

Matt Straw, 19 cm (7.5") high.
Byrne's Fine Art Auctioneers Mar 2004 sold £200
Ebay Jan 2005 sold £316
Est. £400-500

Blue (not pictured), 19.5 cm (7.5") high.
Shapiro Sept 2004 sold AU$1440/£585
Est. £500-700

Vase 4317

Matt Green, 23.5 cm
(9.5") high.
Shapiro Sept 2004
sold AU$1680/£685
Est. £650-850

Image provided courtesy of Shapiro Auctioneers.

Back Row from Left 3991, 3805, 3765, 4317.
Front Row from Left 3820, 3873.

Vase 4318

Moonstone, 19 cm (7") high.
Est. £500-650

Vase 4323

Moonstone, 12.5 cm (5") high.
Ebay Mar 2005 sold £325
Est. £500-650

Vase 4324

Moonstone, 18 cm (7") high.
Ebay Jan 2005 sold £521
Est. £700-850

Vase 4325

Moonstone, 30.5 cm (12") high.
Ebay Mar 2005 sold £191
Est. £300-400

Foreign Currency Rates

Currency rates alter from day to day. On 24/06/2005 the rates were as follows against the GB Pound.

US Dollar	1.82	**Euro**	1.50
Canadian Dollar	2.25	**Australian Dollar**	2.37

A simple calculation to find the daily rate is as follows:

£100 x 1.82 = $182 (US Dollars)
£100 x 2.25 = $225 (Canadian Dollars)
£100 x 1.50 = €150 (Euros)
£100 x 2.37 = $237 (Australian Dollars)

Example: An item costing £120 would be calculated as follows:
£120 x 1.82 (US current rate) = $218.40 in US Dollars.
To find the rate in reverse, divide the rate:

$100 divided	**1.82 = £54.94**	**€100 divided**	**1.50 = £66.67**
$100 Canada	**2.25 = £44.44**	**$100 Australia**	**2.37 = £42.19**

Tableware

Beaker 3885

Black Basalt, 10 cm (4") high.
Ebay Nov 2004 sold £680
Est. £900-1200

Beaker 3888

Black Basalt, 10.5 cm (4") high.
Bonhams Feb 2004 sold £956
Est. £1300-1600

Cocktail Cup 3999

Set of 4 in Moonstone with red
ribbing (not pictured).
Ebay Feb 2005 sold £103
one with small chip
Est. £150-200
Est. £40-50 each

Coffee Pot 3901

Moonstone, 20 cm (7.5") high.
Ebay Mar 2005 sold £110
Est. £150-250

Moonstone with silver handle,
20 cm (7.5") high.
Est. £150-250

Coffee Set

One Moonstone Coffee Pot
One Moonstone Cream Jug
One Moonstone Sugar Box
Four Moonstone Cups and Saucers
Woolley & Wallis Feb 2004 sold £480
Est. £700-1000 the Set

Coffee Pot 3901

Black Basalt, 20 cm (7.5") high.
Ebay Oct 2004 sold £300
Est. £400-500

Cup and Saucer, Coffee 3901

Moonstone.
Ebay Nov 2004 sold £30
Est. £40-60

Moonstone with silver handle
Ebay Nov 2004 sold £26
Ebay Feb 2005 sold £26
Est. £40-60

Matt Green (not pictured).
Ebay Nov 2004 sold £51
Est. £40-60

Comport 4120

Moonstone (not pictured),
23 cm (9") diameter.
Ebay May 2005 sold £99
Est. £150-250

Matt Green, 23 cm (9") diameter.
Ebay Nov 2004 sold £155
Est. £150-250

Jug 3822

Matt Green, 22 cm (8.5") high.
Ebay Jan 2005 sold £69
Ebay Feb 2005 sold £50
Est. £100-150

Matt Straw, 22 cm (8.5") high.
Ebay Oct 2004 sold £77
Est. £100-150

Jug 3844

Matt Straw, 24 cm (9.5") high.
Ebay Oct 2004 sold £39
Est. £100-150

Jug 3845

Matt Straw, 20 cm (8") high.
PSA Sept. 2004 sold £250
Est. £350-450

Jug 3974

Moonstone.
Ebay Oct 2004 sold £38
Est. £60-100

Jug 4193 *(see also 3822)*

Celadon Slipware, 21cm
(8.5") high.
*Lyon & Turnbull Nov 2004
sold £50*
Ebay Feb 2005 sold £43
Est. £70-120

Group of six Celadon Slipware
Mugs (one chipped underneath)
and one Jug.
Ebay Mar 2005 sold £123
Est. £200-300

Mug 3810

Coronation of George VI 1937.
12 cm (4.75") high.
Ebay Feb 2005 sold £50
Ebay Apr 2005 sold £56
Est. £70-100

Mug 3810

Cream, 12 cm (4.75") high
Ebay Feb 2005 sold £29
Ebay Apr 2005 sold £25
Est. £40-70

Moonstone (not pictured),
12 cm (4.75") high.
Ebay Jan 2005 sold £40
Est. £40-70

Matt Straw, 12 cm (4.75") high
Ebay Oct 2004 sold £21
Ebay Nov 2004 sold £29
Est. £40-70

Matt Green, 12 cm (4.75") high
Ebay Jan 2005 sold £41
Ebay Apr 2005 sold £31
Est. £40-70

Mug 3810

The 1940 opening of electrically
fired tunnel oven at Barlaston.
12 cm (4.75") high.
Dreweatt Neate Mar 2004
sold £220
Est. £300-400

Mug 3810

Horse painted by A. Stogdon
12 cm (4.75") high.
Ebay Nov 2004 sold £31
Est. £40-70

Mug 3810

Drawings by C Astley Maberly
12 cm (4.75") high.
Ebay Feb 2005 sold £93
Est. £150-200

Mug *(to match Jug 3844)*

Straw, 12 cm (4.75") high.
Ebay Nov 2004 sold £63
Est. £80-120

Mug 3810

Silver lustre tankard with patterns by Millicent Taplin.
12 cm (4.75") high.
Ebay Nov 2004 sold £84
Christies Feb 2005 sold £180 pair
Ebay Mar 2005 sold £60
Est. £120-160

Mug 3970

Cream, 12.5 cm (5") high.
Ebay Dec 2004 sold £31
Ebay Jan 2005 sold £40
Est. £60-80

Mug 3971

Cream, 14 cm (5.5") high.
Ebay Feb 2005 sold £41
Est. £60-80

Mug 3974

Coronation of Queen Elizabeth II 1953.
Cream with blue, 10 cm (4") high.
Ebay Oct 2004 sold £12
Ebay Mar 2005 sold £8
Est. £15-25

Mug 4192

Slipware Celadon, 12 cm (4.75") high.
Ebay Nov 2004 sold £25
Ebay Jan 2005 sold £41
Est. £60-80

Plate 4122

Matt Green, 20 cm (8") diameter.
Ebay Feb 2005 sold £39
Est. £45-60

Plate with Green Tree pattern by Murray

Moonstone with transfer by KM, 26.5 cm (10.5") diameter.
Ebay Mar 2005 sold £20
Ebay Mar 2005 sold £25
Est. £35-45

Plate for Coronation of Edward VIII

Cream with blue transfers,
31 cm (12") diameter.
*Special Auction Services
Sept 2003 sold £100*
Est. £150-200

Tray 3812

Moonstone, 35 cm (14") diameter.
Ebay Feb 2005 sold £121
Woolley & Wallis May 2005
sold £220
Est. £350-450

Matt Green (not pictured),
35 cm (14") diameter.
(Shapiro Sept 2004
sold AU$600/£243
Est. £350-450

Matt Straw (not pictured),
35 cm (14") diameter.
Ebay Jan 2005 sold £205
Est. £350-450

Blue, 35 cm (14") diameter.
Ebay Dec 2004 sold £300
Est. £450-650

Sugar Box 3901

Matt Green, 9 cm (3.5") high.
Ebay Feb 2005 sold £87
Est. £100-130

Tumbler 3901

Moonstone, 7.5 cm (3") diameter
9 cm (3.5") high.
Ebay Apr 2005
sold AU$81/£33
Ebay Apr 2005
sold £45
Est. £60-70

Bowls

Bowl 3753

Moonstone (not pictured),
16.5 cm (6.5″) high.
Ebay Nov 2004 sold £245
Ebay Jan 2005 sold £161
Est. £350-450

Matt Green, 19 cm (7.5″) high.
Est. £450-550

Matt Straw, 19 cm (7.5″) high.
Ebay Mar 2005 sold £311
Est. £450-550

Matt Straw, 23cm (9″) high.
PSA Sept 2004 sold £260
Est. £450-550

Blue, 11.5 cm (4.5″) high.
Ebay Nov 2004 sold £321
Est. £500-600

Bowl 3806

Moonstone (not pictured), 25.5 cm (10")
diameter 12.5 (5") high.
Ebay Mar 2005 sold £190
Ebay Apr 2005 sold £155
Est. £250-350

Matt Green, 25.5 cm (10") diameter
12.5 (5") high.
Ebay Jan 2005 sold £169
Est. £250-350

Blue, 21.5 cm (8.5") diameter
11.5 (4.5") high.
Ebay Jan 2005 sold £190
Ebay Apr 2005 sold £196
Est. £250-350

Bowl 3813

Moonstone, 16.5 cm (6.5") diameter
10 cm (4") high.
Ebay Oct 2004 sold £192
Est. £250-350

Basalt, 10 cm (4") diameter
6.5 cm (2.5") high.
Shapiro Sept 2004
sold AU$1080/£440
Ebay Mar 2005 sold £515
Est. £750-1000

Bowl 3815

Matt Straw (not pictured),
23.5 cm (10") diameter.
Byrne's Fine Art Auctioneers May 2003 sold £210
Ebay Oct 2004 sold £172
Est. £300-400

Black Basalt Bowl
24.2cm (9.5") diameter.
Christies Feb 2005 sold £480
Est. £750-1000

Bowl 4116

Moonstone, 13 cm (5") high.
Est £200-300

Bowl 3819

Matt Green, 23.5 cm (10")
diameter 12.5 cm (5") high.
Ebay Feb 2005 sold £86
Est. £150-200

Bowl 4126

Moonstone (not pictured), 22 cm (8.5") diameter.
Woolley & Wallis Apr 2004 sold £130
Est. £250-350

Bowl 4129

Moonstone, 27 cm (10.5") diameter
10.5 cm (4") high.
Ebay Oct 2004 sold £157
Est. £200-300

Matt Green (not pictured),
25.5 cm (10") high.
Shapiro Sept 2004 sold AU$480/£197
Est. £200-300

Bowl 4194

Celedon Slipware, 28 cm
(11") diameter 11.5 cm
(4.5") high.
Ebay Oct 2004 sold £95
Est. £150-200

Bowl 4199

Champagne Slipware.
Est. £300-450

Bowl 4200

Champagne Slipware
Ebay Oct 2004 sold £271
Est. £300-450

Bowl 4254

Celadon Slipware, 15 cm (6") high.
Ebay Nov 2004 sold £75
Est. £100-150

Bowl for Coronation

George VI
Cream with blue transfer,
(10.25") wide (4.25") high.
Ebay Nov 2004 sold £126
Est. £200-250

Edward VIII
Cream with blue transfer, (10.25")
wide (4.25") high.
Ebay Mar 2004 sold £200
Est. £250-300

Miscellaneous

Ash Tray 3881

Matt Green.
Ebay Nov 2004 sold £36
Est. £40-60.

Matt Straw.
Ebay Mar 2005 sold £26
Est. £40-60

Bookends

Moonstone.
Est. £200-250

Candlestick 4108

Moonstone, 10 cm (4") diameter 7.5 cm (3") high.
Ebay Nov 2004 sold £38
Ebay Apr 2005 sold £38
Est. £40-60

Auction and Internet Prices

Please remember that Auction House prices carry a buyer's premium.
Today it can be anything from 12 to 20 per cent plus VAT. Therefore
where this book shows a sale at auction, 20 per cent should be added by
the reader to get the true price that the buyer has paid.
Ebay prices do not carry a buyer's premium but the buyer is expected to
pay for the postage and shipping. However, the seller pays a premium
around 4 to 5 per cent on sales. All these facts should be taken into
consideration when arriving at a valuation.

Cigarette Box 3871

Moonstone (not pictured),
19 cm (7.5") wide.
Ebay Mar 2005 sold £148
Est. £200-300

Cigarette Box 4112

Moonstone, 8 cm (20.5") high.
Sworders Oct 2003 sold £340
Est. £500-600

Cigarette Box 3872

Matt Green, 19 cm (7.5") wide 5 cm (2") high.
Ebay Nov 2004 sold £138
Ebay Mar 2005 sold £205
Est. £250-350

Illustration shows the inkstand in pieces. As can be seen from the photograph, the liners would often be stained with blue or red ink.

Inkstand 3873

Moonstone (not pictured),
25.5 cm (10") wide 7 cm (2.75") high.
Cheffins Jan 2003 sold £300
Est. £500-800
(If perfect with lid and liners)

Matt Green, 25.5 cm (10") wide 7 cm (2.75") high.
Ebay Apr 2005 sold £350
Est. £500-800
(If perfect with lid and liners)

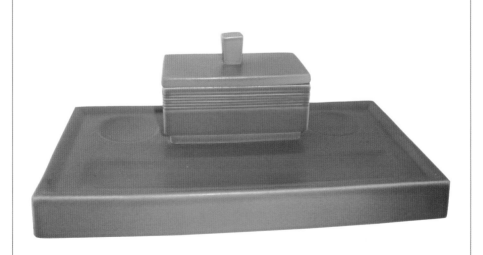

Inkstand 4110

Moonstone, (6.5") wide (9.5") high.
Ebay Apr 2005 sold £210
Est. £300-500
(If perfect with lid and liners)

Inkstand 4131

Desk Stand complete with lid and liner.
Matt green (not pictured),
19 cm (7.5") wide 9 cm (3.5") high.
Bonhams Apr 2005 sold £260
Ebay Apr 2005 sold £295
Est. £400-550
(If perfect with lid and liners)

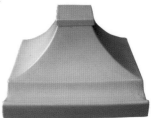

Inkstand

Matt Green
Est. £500-700

Ink-wells were very popular in the 1920s-30s.
Wedgwood produced at least four designs by
Keith Murray in the 1930s, the round version is the
least common.

Inkstand

Moonstone, 25.5 cm (10") wide
10.5 cm (4") high.
Ebay Apr 2005 sold £120
with three small chips
Est. £350-550
(If perfect with lid and liners)

Lamp Vase 3955

Moonstone, , 26 cm (10.25") high.
Ebay Apr 2005 sold £325
Est. £400-600

Matt Green, 26 cm (10.25") high.
Woolley & Wallis May 2005 sold £260
Est. £400-600

Jar, Bath Salts

Moonstone and Matt Green.
Est. £100-150

Lamp Vase 3956

Moonstone.
Est. £400-600

Wall Vase 4141

Matt Green,
20 cm (8") high.
Est. £100-150

Annular Ware

Cup and Saucer

Silver Grey, Cup 6.5 (2.5") high,
Saucer 12.5 (5") diameter.
Ebay Oct 2004 sold £11.50
Est. £12-20

Crescent Plate, Salad

Moonstone, 21.5 cm (8.5")
diameter.
Ebay Jan 2005 sold £10
Est. £10-20

Bowl

Matt Green, 4 cm (1.5") deep
16.5 cm (6.5") diameter.
*Ebay Feb 2004
sold £41 for set of six*
Est. £10-15 each.

Jug

Matt Green, 7 cm (2.5") high.
Ebay Jan 2005 sold £21
Est. £30-40

Oval Dish, Serving

Green, 37 cm (10.5") long
30.5 cm (12") wide.
Ebay Mar 2005 sold £9.50
Est. £15-20

Plate

Moonstone, 26.5 cm (10.5") diameter.
Ebay Oct 2004 sold £16
Est. £20-30

Soup Cup with Twin Handles and Saucer

Silver Grey,
Cup 12.5 cm (5") diameter 5 cm (2") high.
Saucer 17 cm (6.75") diameter.
Ebay Mar 2005 sold £36
Est. £45-55

Tureen

Moonstone (not pictured).
Ebay Oct 2004 sold £57
Est. £65-90

Estimated Valuations

The estimated valuations in this book have been arrived at from a combination of auction and Internet results plus sales made at antique and collectable centres, shops and fairs. It is obvious that bargains can be had from all manner of venues; this is why dealers scour boot fairs and the like. Buyers and collectors should accept that a proprietor of an established business has to pay rent and expenses and his or her sales have to cover those outgoings so a buyer should expect to pay the going price, but you can also expect from this type of establishment genuine and reliable service that will provide provenance and guarantees.

Glass

PRICE GUIDE

Price Guide

Bowl

Clear glass with black foot, 26 cm (10.25") diameter 9 cm (3.75") high.
Ebay Apr 2005 sold £490
Est. £600-900

Decanter with four Glasses

Clear glass with black enamel, 30 cm (12") high.
Woolley & Wallis Feb 2004
sold £200 with chip to stopper
Est. £400-600

Engraved Decanter

Clear glass bevelled spiral, 20 cm (8") high.
See above photograph, item to the left.
Shapiro Sept 2004 sold AU$1200/£492
Est. £600-800

Engraved Vase

Clear glass with floral etching,
20 cm (8") high.
See above photograph,
item in the middle.
*Shapiro Sept 2004
sold AU$840/£344*
Est. £800-1000

Engraved Decanter

698A, clear glass.
See above photograph,
item to the right.
*Shapiro Sept 2004
sold AU$110/£45*
Est. £200-400

Rectangular Decanter

c.1935
20.5cm (8 ins) high
Est. £400-500

Engraved Vase

Clear glass engraved with two fish, weeds and bubbles,
21 cm (8.5") high.
Sotheby's Nov 2001 sold £1,645
Est. £2000-3000

Engraved Vase, 1109A

Clear glass engraved with three cacti, 20 cm (8") high.
Sotheby's Nov 2001 sold £1,762
McTear's Jul 2004 sold £980
Est. £2000-3000

Vase

Free-blown with flared rim.
Overall symmetry and smooth surface.
Est. £250-350

Engraved Vase, 775A

Clear glass engraved cactus,
20.5 cm (8") high.
Lyon & Turnbull Apr 2004 sold £560
Est. £900-1200

Engraved Vase, 946A

Clear glass engraved
cactus, 35cm (14") high.
Dreweatt Neate Nov 2004
sold £780
Est. £1200-1600

'Cactus' Designs

Murray produced a series of Cactus designs for Stevens & Williams
mostly for vases, but a few were used on decanters.

The engraving process is painstakingly long and very arduous. Some
are unmarked and unsigned, but most designs can be found in the
archives of Broadfield House Glass Museum. Examples are quite rare
and highly collectable.

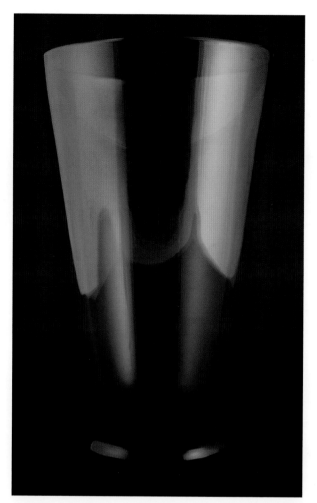

Vase

Green Glass,
31 cm (12.25 ins) high
Woolley & Wallace
May 2005
Estimated £700-1200 unsold
Est. £1000-1200

Cut Bowl

Clear glass.
23 cm (9ins) approx.
diameter
Est. £700-900

Blown Glass

In the 1920s and 1930s the techniques for producing blown glass was an intrinsic element of the simple form that designers such as Keith Murray were trying to achieve.

The method was used in early times and consists of collecting molten glass on the end of a blowing iron, blowing it to the desired size by either free-blowing or into a mould and then turning the glass to create an even surface. The glass is then tranferred to a solid rod known as 'pontil iron' to complete the shaping. It is then removed from the rod to slowly cool down.

Vases

303A

Bottle Green glass conical shape,
31 cm (12") high.
See above photograph, on left.
Shapiro Sept 2004
sold AU$2760/£1133
Est. £1200-1500

412A

Bottle Green glass baluster shape,
39 cm (15.5") high.
See above photograph, centre.
Shapiro Sept 2004
sold AU$2280/£936
Est. £1200-1500

1039

Sapphire blue glass with bubble
decoration, 31 cm (12") high.
See above photograph, on right.
Shapiro Sept 2004
sold AU$2640/£1083
Est. £1200-1500

Vase

Possibly 866A

Bottle Green glass,
21.5 cm (8.5") high.
Woolley & Wallis April 2004
sold £280
Est. £450-650

Vase

Bottle Green glass,
26.5 cm (10.5") high.
Woolley & Wallis
February 2004 sold £380
Est. £600-800

Silver

PRICE GUIDE

Silver & Silver Plate

Keith Murray designed fewer pieces of silver than either pottery or glass, and they sold in smaller numbers at the time. This means it is rare that silver attributed to Murray comes onto the market. As Mappin & Webb did not give these pieces a unique mark, identifying them is not easy and the buyer must carefully judge from their own experience, along with the hallmarks date, before taking a chance on a piece sold unattributed or from an unreliable source

Collection of silver and silver plate are by Mappin & Webb
attributed to Keith Murray designs.
Valuation not known.
Courtesy of Roland Gallery, 33 Monmouth Street, Bath, BA1 2AN.

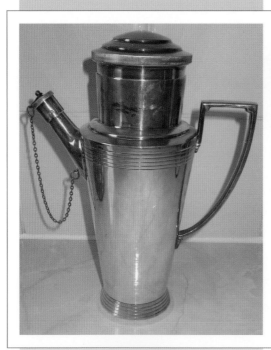

Cocktail Shaker

1930s
Silver plate.
23cm (9ins) high.

Cocktail Shaker

1930s
Silver plate with engavings.
23cm (9ins) high.

Teaset

1938
Silver with Sheffield hallmark.
Teapot 15cm (6ins) high.

DESIGNERS

Associated with Keith Murray

Eric Ravilous

As one of the most prolific designers to work with Wedgwood, Eric Ravilious demonstrated the possibilities of modern design applied to the finest traditions in tableware. Some of his most notable designs were Alphabet nursery ware, Garden, Travel, Persephone and Golden Persephone tableware patterns, and Afternoon Tea teaware. He designed for Wedgwood between 1936 and 1942.

Teapot produced by Wedgwood with the
hand-painted Persephone pattern.
Designed by Eric Ravilious.

Garden mug by Eric Ravilious and a Richard Guyatt mug. Both produced for Wedgwood.
Est. £250-350 pair

Two alphabet mugs produced by Wedgwood from a design by Eric Ravilious.
Est. £200-300 each

John Skeaping

In 1926 John Skeaping sent Wedgwood samples of animal carvings he had made. These were of animals at the London Zoological Gardens. Ten were put into production including a Kangaroo, Buck, Fallow Deer, Bison and Buffalo. They used glazes by Norman Wilson in colours such as Terracotta, Honey Buff, Celadon, Turquoise Blue, Ivory, Cream and Black Basalt.

Sealion designed by John Skeaping for Wedgwood. Est. £200-250

Image provided courtesy of Shapiro Auctioneers.

From top left (clockwise):
Polar Bear by John Skeaping. Est. £1000-1200
Tiger and Buck by John Skeaping. Est. £700-900
Duiker Lying by John Skeaping. Est. £300-400
Silver mounted Fox Head by Wedgwood and Bentley. Est. £500-600

Duiker by John Skeaping for Wedgwood. Est. £200-250

Monkeys designed by John Skeaping for Wedgwood. Est. £200-250

Victor Skellern

Skellern first started at Wedgwood at the age of fourteen, in 1923, serving apprenticeship in the decorating shops and design studios. From this beginning he worked up to the position of Art Director by 1934. He worked closely with other designers and also produced many patterns and shapes himself.

A commemorative mug produced for the move from the Etruria factory to Barlaston in 1940. It was designed by Victor Skellern on a Keith Murray shape.
Dreweatt Neate March 2004 sold £210
Est. £300-400

One of a number of wares introduced by Victor Skellern in the late 50's. These pieces did not carry the designer's name like Keith Murray's did and at times have been confused with his. It is approximately 11 cm (4.25") high and 26 cm (10.25") wide, with a moonstone glaze.

Millicent Taplin

Millicent Taplin was a skilled artist who was employed at Wedgwood between 1917 and 1962, first in the hand-painting department and by 1955 as Head of the Wedgwood School of freehand painters. She created many designs for Wedgwood ranging from handpainted ones to lithographic designs developed with Victor Skellern.

Image provided courtesy of Shapiro Auctioneers.

A hand painted floral pattern by Millicent Taplin for Wedgwood. This is one of a number of shapes by Keith Murray which she used.
Roseberrys March 2005
sold £210
Est. £250-300

Wall Plaque c.1945

A pattern with rooster at the centre by Millicent Taplin for Wedgwood.
Shapiro Australia Sept 2004
sold $AU3360/£1366
Est. £1000-1500

Norman Wilson

In 1927 Norman Wilson joined Wedgwood on the request of Major Frank Wedgwood. He made a name for himself as a skilled technician and experimenter. His experiments resulted in many new glazes which Wedgwood were to exploit, such as those used by Keith Murray. He also worked as a designer, helping to create new shapes for the company. Between 1928 and 1963 he produced a considerable number of unique wares. The term "unique" was used to describe the unpredictable nature of their glazes. These were not sold through the usual channels, but through private collections and exhibitions.

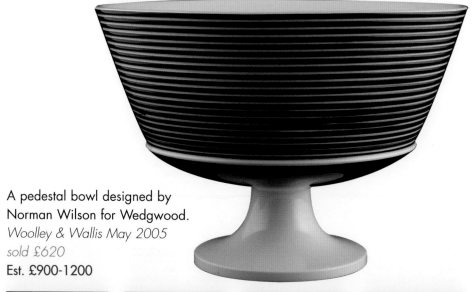

A pedestal bowl designed by Norman Wilson for Wedgwood.
Woolley & Wallis May 2005
sold £620
Est. £900-1200

Woolley & Wallis	*Woolley & Wallis*	*Woolley & Wallis*	*Woolley & Wallis*
April 2003	*Feb 2004*	*Feb 2004*	*Feb 2004*
sold £130	*sold £190*	*sold £280*	*sold £420*
Est. £200-300	**Est. £300-350**	**Est. £450-550**	**Est. £650-800**

Internet and Auctions Based in the UK

www.ebay.co.uk

Most internet users know of the auction website Ebay. In recent years it has taken off at a tremendous rate and is currently selling more goods by auction than any other site. Many collectors and dealers are using Ebay today and are finding that it supplements their other outlets which cannot be a bad thing. If you haven't tried it before then you can find pieces by Keith Murray by typing his name into search box and selecting the Ceramics & Glass category beside it; this will bring up a list of items currently being sold.

Auction Houses

Bonhams	www.bonhams.com
Cheffins	www.cheffins.co.uk
Christies	www.christies.com
Dreweatt Neate	www.dnfa.com
Fellows & Sons	www.fellows.co.uk
Gorringes	www.gorringes.co.uk
Law Fine Art	www.lawfineart.co.uk
McTear's	www.mctears.com
Peter Wilson	www.peterwilson.co.uk
Potteries Specialist Auctions (PSA)	www.potteriesauctions.com
Rosebery's	www.roseberys.co.uk
Sotheby's	search.sothebys.com
Sworders	www.sworder.co.uk
Woolley & Wallis	www.woolleyandwallis.co.uk

Antiques Fairs

Alexandra Palace	www.allypally-uk.com
Ann Zierold Fairs	www.annzieroldfairs.co.uk
Art Deco Fairs from Abbey Fairs	www.artdeco-fairs-warwick.com
DecoFairs, Brighton & Hove & London Art Deco Fair	020 8663 3323
Olympia Fine Arts and Antiques Fairs	www.olympia-antiques.com
UK Antique Fairs from Take Five Fairs	www.antiquefairs.co.uk

Bibliography

20th Century Ceramic Designers in Britain, Casey, A., 2001, Antique Collectors' Club

Wedgwood Ceramics 1846-1959, Batkin, M., 1982, Richard Dennis

British Glass Between the Wars, Dodsworth, R. (ed.), 1987, Dudley Leisure Services.

The Design of Table Glass (article), Design for Today, Murray, K., 1933

Drawings of Spain (exhibition catalogue), Murray, K., 1928, Alex. Reid & Lefèvre, Ltd.

International Modern Glass, Beard, G., 1976, Barrie and Jenkins.

Keith Murray (exhibition catalogue), Hawkins, J., 1987, Victoria & Albert Museum

Keith Murray Modern Glass - The Swedish Connection (article), The Journal, Taylor, D., 1987, The Glass Association

Pottery Pure and Simple (article), Art & Antiques, Crossingham-Gower, G., 1976

Unpublished interview between R. Dodsworth and S. Thompson, 2001

Wedgwood Catalogue of Bodies, Glazes and Shapes Current for 1940-1950, 1947, Josiah Wedgwood & Sons

INDEX